ONTARIO

ONTARIO

Photographed and written by J. A. Kraulis

Whitecap Books
North Vancouver, B.C.

Canadian Cataloguing in Publication Data

Kraulis, J. A., 1949-
   Ontario

   ISBN 0-920620-32-9

   1. Ontario — Description and travel —
Views. I. Title.
FC3062.K73   917.13'044'0222   C82-091330-8
F1057.8.K73

Copyright © Whitecap Books Ltd.

First edition 1982

Published by
**Whitecap Books Limited,
Ste 1, 431 Mountain Highway,
North Vancouver, B.C.
V7J 2L1**

Printed in Canada

Credits

Designed by Michael Burch

Printed and bound by D. W. Friesen and Sons Ltd.

Colour separations by Jack Berger Ltd.

Aerial photography on pages 30, 36, 37, 56, 66, 67, 78, 82 and 85 co-produced with Bo Curtis

Photographs on pages 46 (top) 47, and 73 by Gera Dillon.

An Introduction to the Province of Ontario

Ontario is a land that defies brief and summary description. It is a land where polar bears roam along a barren saltwater coast in the north, but where vine-choked jungle thrives on a freshwater coast in the south. In Killarney Provincial Park overlooking Georgian Bay, it is a coarse, bumpy land with a surface of unyielding granite and white quartzite ridges; but not far away, in the Holland Marsh, it is a smooth flat land, soft and thick with some of the richest black soil in Canada. In Sarnia, Sudbury and Hamilton, refineries, smelters and mills belch noise and smoke and resemble enormous modernistic stage sets of hell; in contrast, Algonquin Provincial Park is a paradise of fresh breezes and pine-scented tranquility, an opera house for the haunting songs of the loon and the whip-poor-will. The outskirts of Toronto are paved over with myriad roads feeding twelve-lane superhighways and buzzing, bewildering interchanges; while one could as easily get lost canoeing thousands of kilometres of water routes devoid of any trace of man in the outlying region of Quetico Provincial Park, Lake of the Woods and northward. The "Golden Horseshoe", the commercial and industrial end of Lake Ontario, is the most crowded real estate in Canada, while in the Hudson Bay Lowlands in the north, one could easily find oneself 100 kilometres removed from the next closest human being. The cities of Ontario are constantly changing, burgeoning with new imaginative monuments of modern architecture; but time seems to have passed by many of the backroad towns with their old greystone buildings and occasional hand-operated canal locks, towns such as Merrickville, Elora and Pakenham to name a few. Ontario is a complex and sophisticated land, home to an amazing diversity of human enterprise and culture; it is also a basic, elemental land dominated by stone, water and wood.

There is no simple way to describe Ontario. Its salient geographic features, its people and their activities constitute a mosaic and a maze. A glance at a road map readily demonstrates the latter. The relatively small area between Toronto and Ottawa is a puzzle of so many different alternate routes that one could spend a lifetime driving back and forth between the two cities and never travel exactly the same path more than once. This is even more true for the province's natural water routes.

A closer study of the map provides a hint of the cultural mosaic of Ontario.

Brussels, Paris, London, Zurich, Vienna, Moscow, Washington, Florence, Copenhagen, Gibraltar, Damascus, Hanover, Dublin, Warsaw, Athens, Melbourne: all are the place names of existing towns in Ontario, which even has a Mississippi, a Thames and a Seine River, not to mention a community called Eden. The English roots of the first settlers are everywhere evident in hundreds of names from Avon to York, while the most evocative and descriptive names are indisputably those of native Indian origin: Kapuskasing, Temagami, Nipissing, Kakabeka, Manitoulin, Keewatin, Mississauga, Wawa, Niagara, Kanata and, not the least, the names of the province itself and of its two capital cities.

A land of diversity and contrast such as Ontario is not readily divisible into distinct regions, but the province can be thought of in terms of its northern, southern and eastern sections, with a geographical and historic centre around Georgian Bay, the Land of the Hurons.

By far the greatest portion of the land area of the province is occupied by the region generally referred to as Northern Ontario, which in a strict sense usually means everything north and west of North Bay, but which in terms of the character of the land takes in the Ottawa valley west of Ottawa and regions as far south as Algonquin Park. Even in its narrowly defined sense, it occupies nearly nine-tenths of the province, taking in all of its west and, in geographic terms, leaving little space for other regions. In area, it is much larger than any European nation outside of the Soviet Union.

Northern Ontario is big country, a generous home for the moose and oversize fish which are so abundant here. Black bears prowl much of its timberland down to its southern portions and polar bears patrol its barren northernmost fringe along the arctic coastline of Hudson Bay in Polar Bear Provincial Park.

It is a place with room for many big lakes, including the biggest of them all, Lake Superior. One of Canada's largest ports is located on Superior's shore, 4000 kilometres from the ocean. Thunder Bay, its harbour lined with the greatest array of grain elevators in existence, marks the transfer point of western Canada's harvest from train to ship.

The size and remoteness of Northern Ontario is underscored by the fact that, while it is accessible to ocean-going ships, much of it can only be reached by float planes. Over vast areas, the only trace of human settlement is an occasional hunting or fishing lodge or a trapper's cabin.

Northern Ontario is far from being pristine, unbroken wilderness, however; it is also the home of some giants of industry. Here the mine headframe and the smokestack are as common as the prairie grain elevator is to the west. Thick relentless plumes of smoke signal the location of pulp mills and smelters, abundant evidence of the wealth of the Canadian Shield, a broad, heavy money belt that sags across

Ontario's widest section. Here money grows in billions of trees and is sealed in vaults of stone. In both pulpwood and in minerals, Ontario's Shield is an exceptionally productive region.

The most impressive of the big businesses is prominently on display at Sudbury. The world's tallest smokestack, higher than all but a half dozen skyscrapers, marks the location of a mine and a smelter which, each year from 1905 until very recently, was by itself the source of more than half of the world supply of nickel, and which is still the greatest source of the white metal. Here the land has been turned inside out in a vast expanse of multi-coloured tailings. Underneath burrow the tunnels which have, in addition to nickel, yielded significant quantities of copper, silver, platinum, palladium, cobalt, sulfur and iron.

Other northern mining communities also boast international records. Timmins has the richest silver-zinc mine, while Elliot Lake has the largest known deposit of uranium.

In a nation where vastness is the rule, Northern Ontario is still noted for its distances. To the traveller who undertakes to drive the Trans-Canada Highway, the section through this area will be the most remembered, simply for its sheer duration. By the time one reaches North Bay heading west, one has already spent a good day of driving through the province, yet two more long days lie ahead before the Shield country finally flattens out onto the prairies. Northern Ontario is big enough for two official Trans-Canada Highways, route 17 and the alternate route 11, but no matter which road is chosen, it takes very nearly as much time to cross this undulating, seemingly endless land of lakes and forest as it takes to go from Winnipeg to Vancouver.

And yet the highways are timid visitors to this formidable land, venturing little further than its southern edge. To the north spreads the great spruce sea, the boreal forest, and still further north lie the cold swamps of the Hudson Bay Lowlands. Finally, barren-lands, some of the southernmost arctic tundra on earth, lead to the limestone shores of Hudson Bay.

Southern Ontario is in many ways the opposite of its northern counterpart. Where the latter is characterized by long distances between towns, the former is a veritable forest of cities; within an hour's drive of Metro Toronto alone are a dozen other major urban centres. Much of the north wears a dark, uniform blanket of spruce. The south, on the other hand, is a patched quilt of gardens and woodlots, endless in their variety rather than in expanse. Where most of Northern Ontario rests on a durable granite foundation, most of Southern Ontario is built on limestone, most prominently evident in the 450-kilometre-long Niagara Escarpment running from Niagara Falls to Tobermory. The softer rock yields soil more readily than the hard stone of the Shield, and in Southern Ontario, where once majestic forests ruled, neatly kept farm fields now dominate the landscape where it has been left unclaimed by the numerous expanding cities and smaller towns.

Geographically characteristic of a large portion of Canada, Northern Ontario occupies the waist of the country. While Southern Ontario, with its great share of the population, is seldom thought of as isolated, it is one of the unusual, atypical corners of the land. It is, indeed, an island, not only in terms of its distinctiveness, but in actual fact, for it is impossible to leave Southern Ontario without crossing water. Lakes Ontario, Erie and Huron bound it on three sides, while the Trent-Severn Waterway, a route for recreation boats which connects a number of lakes and rivers with canals, completes the circle to the north.

Perhaps nowhere is the unique separateness of Southern Ontario more manifest than at Point Pelee, a peninsula that terminates in a dagger-shaped sand spit thrusting into Lake Erie. At this southernmost tip of the Canadian mainland, the sky can turn black almost instantly with the heavy clouds of a rapidly advancing storm front. Looking out over the long menacing line of white water where breakers from opposite directions crash into each other, one has the very real and haunting feeling that this is indeed one of the far corners of Canada.

Beyond Point Pelee lies Pelee Island, which also terminates in a long narrow spit pointing into a line of breakers. Not far off, small, uninhabited Middle Island marks the southernmost extension of Canadian territory.

Knifing far out into Lake Erie, Point Pelee acts as a migratory funnel for tens of thousands of monarch butterflies, which every autumn use the point and Pelee Island as their last resting place before the hazardous crossing of the lake. In the evenings towards the end of September, one can sometimes find trees completely covered with butterflies, as numerous as leaves.

The area is also along the migratory route of many exotic species of birds, and the marsh in Point Pelee National Park is one of the best bird watching spots on the continent. Here too grows the Carolinean forest, an ecological immigrant from the southern United States. Tall, densely-leafed deciduous trees with thick vines dangling from their broad canopies, crowd around secret ponds where the great blue heron often stalks. To surprise one of these enormous slow-flapping birds in this exotic setting is to feel how out of character with the rest of Canada this area is. The mood is more evocative of a South American jungle.

Point Pelee is as far south as California and Rome, and like these two regions, it is a grape-growing area. The grapes of Pelee are wild, but northeast, in the Niagara Peninsula, cultivated grapes and wine making is serious business, along with the growing of other fruits such as peaches and cherries. The region closer to Pelee itself grows more vegetables — it accounts for nearly three-quarters of Canada's entire harvest. Leamington, the closest town to the point, is known as the "Tomato Capital of the World". All roads lead to the cannery for the dump trucks, loaded with high piles of the bright red fruit.

The land between the Niagara region and the area north of Pelee is Canada's tobacco capital, centered in Norfolk County. Dairy farms and fields of grain, particularly corn, take over at latitudes north of Toronto, with the notable exception of Holland Marsh, a flat patch of rich black soil at Bradford south of Lake Simcoe.

Farmland has replaced the forests where valuable species such as oak, hickory and walnut were once common, but Southern Ontario still has patches of the deciduous forest region, unique in Canada. Almost entirely devoid of conifers, the region supports scores of different hardwood species, including many which are found nowhere else in the country, such as the tulip-tree, cucumber-tree, red mulberry, black gum, blue ash, black oak, pin oak, sassafras, pawpaw, Kentucky coffee-tree, mockernut hickory and pignut hickory. Contributing to Canada's richest mix of tree species are several other oaks, black walnut, sycamore, beech, basswood, sugar maple, white elm, red ash and butternut.

In absolute contrast to Southern Ontario's pastoral scenes of neat farms and peaceful woodlots is its awesome display of giant industries.

The eerie crackling buzz of high voltage electricity runs through cables which leave the nuclear power plants at Pickering and at Douglas Point, two of the largest anywhere in the world.

Chemical Valley is the complex of refineries at Sarnia where terminates the long pipeline that siphons oil and gas from the rich fields of Alberta. Surrealistically illuminated at night with green industrial lights and sporadic flareups of orange flame, the hissing network of shiny tubes and pipes never sleeps. Chemical Valley is a witch's brewery of Canada's greatest petrochemical industries, its largest fiberglass, synthetic rubber, carbon black and glycol plants, as well as some of the largest oil refineries.

Chemical Valley is the logical successor to North America's first commercial oil field discovered over a hundred years ago at nearby Petrolia. This small Ontario town, today with a population of only 4,000 people, was the home of the first Oil Exchange and was the place where the methods of the oil industry were originally developed and exported to the major fields around the globe.

As awesome and unreal as Sarnia's waterfront along the St. Clair River, Hamilton's steaming mills are correspondingly the country's largest in the iron and steel industry. The Steel Capital of Canada is at the middle of a strip of manufacturing centres from Peterborough to Windsor which are largely responsible for the fact that Ontario produces more manufactured goods than the rest of Canada combined. Machinery, fabricated metals, electrical products industries, and all manner of other industries that depend on these, depend in turn on the blast furnaces at Hamilton, as does especially the automobile industry, the province's largest. Every minute, a vehicle comes off the assembly lines at Oshawa, Brampton, Oakville and Windsor.

Ontario owes its concentration of factories to the world's greatest inland waterway, the Great-Lakes-St. Lawrence Seaway system which connects the province with the central United States on the one hand and Western Canada on the other. Ships from around the world visit Ontario ports, while the local parade of lakers constitutes the bulk of the traffic, shuttling grain to the lower St. Lawrence and Labrador iron ore back upstream to Hamilton.

Simply in terms of spectacle, the man-made portions of the waterway are perhaps Ontario's most interesting industrial attraction. Across the Niagara Peninsula steps a stairway for giants, the Welland Canal. Here big boats, some the length of several football fields and as tall as a medium-sized office building, line up to take their turn at climbing a steep ladder of locks.

The Welland Canal bypasses one of the grandest of spectacles, the source of a most impressive sound. It is a sound that reached the first explorers who ventured up the St. Lawrence, a sound translated into rumours that drifted downstream in the strange language of the Iroquois. The rumours described "Oniagara", the Great Thunderer. Today, the ceaseless drumroll of Niagara Falls resonates in the memories of the many millions who have seen it, and in the imaginations of many more millions who have yet to see it.

Niagara's first tourist, Father Louis Hennepin, heard the falls two days before he arrived on the edge of the cliff overlooking the roaring silver shroud. Or so we must assume, for he described the falls as being two hundred metres high with a din that could be heard more than fifty kilometres away. Properly awed, he exaggerated the facts, but not his impressions, by a factor of four.

The deafening flood of Niagara is an appropriate overture to the voluminous activity, the human beehive, that is Southern Ontario. Within its relatively narrow confines live as many people as in all of Western Canada combined. The depository of much of Ontario's culture, past and future, Southern Ontario has innumerable museums and most of the province's fifteen universities.

The museums include many historic homes which on a small scale preserve the lifestyle of a period or the memory of a famous citizen, or both. The Laura Secord Homestead in Queenston was the dwelling of the famous Canadian heroine who overheard American troops during the war of 1812 plotting an attack, and who delivered the strategically vital information to the British by making an epic thirty-kilometre trek across swamps and through dense bush. The home of Alexander Graham Bell in Brantford commemorates one of North America's greatest inventors. Guelph maintains the Colonel John McCrea Home, birthplace of the man who is best known for his poem, "In Flanders Fields".

These homes are like fine appetizers, delightful and entirely worthwhile for their own sake, too numerous for one appetite on the one hand but mere tidbits on a sumptuous tray on the other. Southern Ontario, like most of the rest of the province, is full of larger museums, many of them in old churches, schools, mills or other renovated buildings. They cover every conceivable subject, from pioneer life to high technology, from military history to that of the many native bands who live in the province, from fine art to the collection of antique cars in the Canadian Automotive Museum in Oshawa.

Some of the well-kept towns of Ontario are living museums. Niagara-on-the-Lake, once the capital of Ontario when it was called Newark and the province was Upper Canada, preserves its elegance in the façades of Nineteenth Century shops and inns along its broad main street.

However, it is in the present that Southern Ontario's culture is most lively and conspicuous — in its theatres, its concert halls, its exhibitions, its festivals. The Shaw Festival at Niagara-on-the-Lake and the Stratford Festival with its rich Shakespearean program present the work of two of the English language's greatest playwrights. More home-grown festivals celebrate the seasons and local ethnic roots: the Maple Syrup Festival in Elmira, Kleinburg's Binder Twine Festival in the autumn, the Blossom Festival of Niagara Falls, the Highland Games in Cambridge and Fergus, and Oktoberfest in Kitchener-Waterloo.

Much of the scattered ethnic and economic diversity of Southern Ontario is centred in Toronto. Its name means "Meeting Place" and it is indeed a gathering spot. Circled by jetliners and expressways, the busy centre is the inevitable place towards which both business and entertainment gravitate.

Boasting a magnificent skyline dominated by a cluster of black, gold, silver-green and white towers of bank headquarters, Toronto is a showcase of architecture, modern and old.

Among the most elegant of the office skyscrapers is the Royal Bank Building. With its multiangled glass walls impregnated with gold dust and its twin towers vaulting a great interior lobby, it demonstrates what confident design can achieve. Nearby, marble-clad First Canadian Place is the tallest office building in the British Commonwealth.

Toronto is the appropriate capital of Ontario, and the Provincial Parliament Buildings, dating from the late Nineteenth Century, form an imposing mass at the north end of University Avenue. Elaborately carved from red sandstone and granite, they are a vivid contrast to the nearby floating blue glass façade of the Ontario Hydro Building. Like some giant fun mirror in an amusement park, the curved wall of the latter captures a distorted image of its surroundings.

The municipal government buildings are perhaps the most impressive public architecture in Toronto. The modern city hall is a Toronto landmark. Set on an elevated pad overlooking the concrete plain of Nathan Phillips Square, its twin curved shells cradle the flying-saucer of the council chamber like two Jovian launch towers. To the east of the square, the romanesque Old City Hall is an architectural masterpiece from an earlier time.

The satellite boroughs around Toronto also have high architectural standards in their municipal buildings. The bright white twin wedges of the Scarborough Civic Centre meet in a spacious, exciting interior atrium. The sloping front of the North York Civic Centre skylights a similar multi-tiered open interior. The architectural theme in both cases is open accessible government.

Both these buildings contribute to an emerging tradition of inspiring interior public spaces. Other examples include the skylit multilevel shopping galleria of the Eaton Centre and the airy atrium of the Metro Library which allows for a restful and impressive view of the entire interior from any floor.

Ruling Toronto like some heroic arm and sword raised skyward, the CN Tower is a monument to the communications and tourist industries. The tower, the tallest self-supporting structure in the world, is remarkable not only for its height, but for its innovative and superior design. Europe bristles with similar communications towers, each with its revolving restaurant and observation deck, but all have plain tubular shafts. The CN Tower, in elegant contrast, consists of three long tapering buttresses surrounding a central core, hexagonal in cross section, a form which allows for exterior elevators on the flat surfaces as well as for a bracket system to support the seven-story pod. This in turn makes possible the unique openings in the base of the pod which permit a vertiginous view straight down the shaft of the tower.

As exciting as Toronto is, with its architecture, its entertainments and its active harbour front, perhaps no aspect of the city is quite as remarkable as its amazing ethnic diversity. It is conspicuously manifest during celebrations such as Caribana, with its jumping West Indian Parade moving to the rhythm of steel drums, but Metro International Caravan is the ultimate festival, an annual nine-day event organized around the theme pavilion of more than fifty cultures resident in Toronto.

Toronto has one of the continent's largest Chinatowns, and in its restaurants and delicatessens one can buy the best of Polish sausage, Indian curry, German sauerkraut, Estonian sweet and sour bread, Greek salad, Japanese sushi, to name only a very few examples. Altogether, more than eighty different ethnic groups are significantly represented in Toronto. Of the population of 2,849,000 (Canada's largest city), more than half were born outside the country.

Like Southern Ontario, Eastern Ontario is located on a peninsula (or, in part, on a canal-created island), but it is defined by great rivers rather than by great lakes. The two converging rivers are the natural entrances and exits of the province. To the north, the Ottawa River was the path of the first European explorers — Champlain and his associates — who entered what is now Ontario. During the Seventeenth and Eighteenth Centuries, this river was the vital artery of the fur trade. Later, in the Nineteenth Century, it served as a conveyor for outbound timber rafts by which the white pine harvested from its valley was sent downstream to be shipped to Europe. The white pine and the fur-bearing animals are rare now, and the transport function of the river has been transferred to its valley, through which runs the Trans-Canada highway and railroad.

The St. Lawrence River, on the south, is the present-day water entrance to the province. The route of ships carrying international cargoes of every description, it is vital to the commerce of Ontario. It is paralleled by Ontario's most important highway, Route 401, the MacDonald-Cartier Freeway, which links Toronto and Montreal.

Overlooking both rivers are past and present national capitals. Kingston, guarding the entrance to the St. Lawrence where the river leaves Lake Ontario, is the former capital of the United Provinces of Canada. Its legacy from those days includes one of the finest works of classical architecture in the country, the building which is now the Kingston City Hall. Another building of note is the Bellevue House, once the residence of Sir John A. MacDonald, Canada's first prime minister.

The most conspicuous of Kingston's historical structures also serves as a reminder of why the city did not remain the capital of Canada. Each summer at Fort Henry, red-coated militiamen act out a noisy imitation of the past in demonstrating the fine points of cannon and musket warfare. Following the war of 1812, Fort Henry was the mightiest of numerous forts built by the British along Ontario's southern water border with the United States. Formidable as the fort was, Kingston still seemed vulnerable to a possible American attack from across the St. Lawrence River.

The Rideau Canal, from Kingston to the Ottawa River, had been completed in 1832, also as a safeguard against a possible American invasion. Bytown, located at the northern terminus of the Rideau Canal and named for the colonel responsible for the canal's construction, was soon chosen as the site of the nation's capital and renamed Ottawa.

Today Ottawa's function as the capital of Canada is evidenced by its many monumental buildings. Parliament Hill, its copper-capped Gothic peaks an architectural version of the Rockies, is one of Canada's most familiar landmarks. Except for the fine library at the back, its Centre Block doesn't look exactly the way it might have; the original edifice was destroyed by fire in 1916. The new building incorporated a taller, more slender central summit, the Peace Tower, which provides a commanding view of the city and is dedicated as a memorial to Canada's war dead.

Nearby is the most permanent-looking building in Ottawa, the rock-like Supreme Court of Canada, solid and unshakeable in appearance. Across the street, the newcomer Bank of Canada Building shows perfect manners, wearing a modest hat of the same weathered copper as its eminent neighbours and sporting a tasteful green glass suit that reflects and complements its setting rather than attracting attention to itself.

To the east of the showcase buildings in Ottawa are the private quarters: 24 Sussex Drive, the Prime Minister's official residence; the palatial Rideau Hall and its spacious grounds, home of the Governor General of Canada; and an impressive gathering of grand mansions housing embassies and foreign government residences.

Due west from the province's eastern gateways, and between Northern and Southern Ontario, lies the region which was nearly the cradle of the province's history and which still best sums up the essence of original Ontario: the region around Georgian Bay, once the land of the Hurons.

At Midland is the wood stockade of Sainte-Marie-Among-the-Hurons, a reconstruction of the only European settlement in Ontario older than the late Eighteenth Century. Here, in the early 1600s, Jesuit missionaries established the first farm, hospital, school and social service in Ontario, as well as the first canal in North America. The efforts of the missionaries came to nought when, as a consequence of the war between the Iroquois and Hurons, the defeated Hurons were forced to leave their land. Along with them went the missionaries who had survived the massacres that had martyred five of their priests. Huronia fell silent and deserted in 1650.

Had the Ste. Marie mission survived, Ontario's history of settlement would be twice as long as it is and most likely very different. Sudbury might be called Brûléville, after Étienne Brûlé who, after travelling westward via the Ottawa River, became the first European to see the Great Lakes when he came to the north end of Georgian Bay. The bay itself would perhaps retain Champlain's original name for it, "La Mer Douce", the Freshwater Sea. As it turned out, the prosperity and culture that thrive in Ontario today had to wait another 150 years before the American Revolution forced the United Empire Loyalists northward to settle along the shores of the Upper St. Lawrence and the Lower Great Lakes.

The wilderness around Georgian Bay has another deep claim on the heritage of Ontario. It is an area indelibly painted into Canada's national identity by that loose association of highly individualistic artists who have been fondly pigeonholed for eternity as the Group of Seven. More farsighted than most, they hiked and canoed into the remote regions of the country to interpret what they saw as Canada's most valuable heritage, the untamed land itself, vast, wild and wondrous. It was in the wildlands around Georgian Bay that they had their beginnings and created much of their famous work, exploring the lonely wood-screened lakes towards Muskoka and Algonquin Park, and wandering the wind wasted pine shores of the Bay itself.

The most profound and far-reaching aspect of Ontario's past is carved into the rock itself. Along the stone shores of eastern Georgian Bay and on every one of its Thirty Thousand Islands there is prominent evidence of the grinding, gouging work of the great ice sheet, three kilometres deep, that once compressed the land. The stone is still slowly rising up from the immense burden it bore a mere hundred human lifetimes ago. When the ice retreated, the Great Lakes and the St. Lawrence River were born, and Niagara Falls began its slow retreat up its precipitous gorge.

The glaciers left behind a feature which all the varied regions of Ontario share — water. No other region on earth is more generously endowed with fresh water. It covers one-sixth of the surface of the province, an area the size of England plus Wales and a good portion of Scotland, an area larger than seventy-five of the world's nations.

The lakes of Ontario claim a giant share of world records. Superior is the largest freshwater lake, Wasaga is the longest freshwater beach, the Thirty Thousand Islands are the greatest freshwater archipelago and Manitoulin is the largest freshwater island. It even has its own islands on its own lakes! So abundantly is Ontario blessed with water that the names of many of its associated features are considerably understated. Regarding the Thousand Islands, there are 1,768 of them. Thirty Thousand Islands sounds like an exaggeration, but there are over 97,000 of them. The 14,632 islands in the beautiful lake that anchors the lower western corner of the land have been ignored; the place is simply Lake of the Woods.

All the statistics say nothing of the sheer beauty of Ontario's water. This is the land of water black and bottomless, and wild and white, wind-torn water silver in the sun and brilliant blue water under a cloudless sky. Here is water green with bands of yellow shoals when seen from above, and soaked orange, gold, pink and red under the sky of a Huron sunset. It is still and invisible, a mirror for every colour that exists on a sunny autumn Muskoka day, and in winter it is immobile and solid, cast in whorled designs of turquoise and grey. In spring it is a relentless explosion when it bursts into life, casting off its heavy white winter quilt.

The lakes and rivers which are the legacy of the Ice Age are also embedded in the more recent history of the province, as exploration and settlement took place along these waterways. Today Ontario's water is not only important to industry and tourism, but to the enjoyment of the people of Ontario, who take advantage of the recreational opportunities offered by the more than a quarter of a million lakes which cover the province. It is not surprising then that this vast, beautiful and complex land takes its name from the water. It is named for just one lake, Ontario, which means "Handsome Lake", an apt description not only for this and a myriad other lakes, but for the province as a whole. Ontario — a handsome land — rich with natural wealth, history and the cultural mosaic which ensures a vital future.

The Trillium, the official provincial flower.

Below and opposite: The beauty of a new spring season in rural Ontario.

Following pages: Fenelon Falls, "The Jewel of the Kawathas", in morning calm along the Trent-Severn Waterway.

Above: Thousands of tulips are planted each year at Dows Lake in Ottawa for the Festival of Spring.

Opposite: The winning design of an international competition, Toronto's City Hall has become one of the province's most famous landmarks.

Above: The world's largest collection of sculptor Henry Moore's work is displayed in a wing of its own at the Art Gallery of Ontario in Toronto.

Opposite: Old and new architecture: University of Toronto buildings with the CN Tower in the background.

Above: Locks on the Rideau Canal descend to the Ottawa River.

Opposite: The Peace Tower dominates the weathered bronze and copper landmarks on Parliament Hill in Ottawa.

Above: A guide in period costume waits at the entrance to one of the many 19th century homes in Upper Canada Village at Morrisburg.

Opposite: Martello Towers guard the entrance to the strategic water passages around Kingston.

Above: The marina at Ontario Place is one of many crowding the Toronto waterfront.

Opposite: Midway rides on the grounds of the Canadian National Exhibition. The exhibition is the largest event of its kind in the world.

Following pages: The skyline of Toronto from Ward's Island.

Above: Generous in area and in number of species, the Metro Toronto Zoo has one of the largest herds of elephants in any zoo in the world.

Opposite: The towns of central Ontario are graced with countless fine old stone buildings. This one houses the public library in Arnprior.

Above: The National Yacht Club in Toronto.

Opposite: The great horseshoe of Niagara Falls is, for good reason, the most photographed place in the world.

Above: The curved glass wall of the Ontario Hydro Building on University Avenue in Toronto.

Opposite: The skylit gallery of the Eaton Centre, Toronto's prime retail showcase.

Following pages: One of the many cascading streams of the Canadian Shield, this one flows into Calabogie Lake.

Above: Dundurn Castle in Hamilton was once the residence of Sir Allan Napier McNab, Prime Minister of the United Provinces of Canada.

Opposite: Past and present contrast in this view of Toronto's Old City Hall and one of the two towers of the new Eaton Centre.

Above: Common but magnificent, Canada Geese are especially abundant in Ontario. The town of Wawa has been named for the migrating birds, while a large population has elected to make the lakeshore in Toronto a year round home.

Opposite: En route to Mexico for the winter, Monarch Butterflies rest on Pelee Island before crossing Lake Erie.

Above: One of many fine performances at Stratford.

Below: Toronto's Italian community celebrate their nation's victory at the 1982 World Cup Soccer competition.

Above: Cultural celebrations in Ontario can involve many different groups from Mennonite to Chinese.

Below: A Lithuanian dance group performs in a Toronto park.

Above: The C.N. Tower provides a sensational view of Toronto at night.

Opposite: Downtown Toronto and the C.N. Tower from the Lakeshore Boulevard.

Preceding pages: The Ottawa River and the Parliament Buildings in the nation's capital.

Above: The smokestacks of a chemical plant in Cornwall.

Opposite: The sun sets on the mills of Hamilton, the steel capital of Canada.

Above: The Holland Marsh, a flat plain of rich black soil, is a busy market garden in a region of dairy and grain farming.

Opposite: Tomatoes by the thousand being processed at the Heinz plant in Leamington.

Fuel for the province: hydro-electric pylons at sunset near Cornwall (*above*), and a petroleum refinery on the shore of Lake
Ontario at Oakville (*opposite*).

Above and opposite: Rural areas become a mass of colour as fall approaches. These scenes are taken in the Muskoka area and on St. Joseph's Island.

Above: Cattle grazing along a dyke separating the Iroquois Canal from the St. Lawrence near Johnstown.

Opposite: Nineteenth century shops contribute their tidy façades to the elegant main street of Niagara-on-the-Lake.

Above: Lakers on Lake Erie are part of a never ending parade of ships on the Great Lakes-St. Lawrence Waterway.

Opposite: Shipyards at Port Weller, the Lake Ontario entrance to the Welland Canal.

Following pages: A variety of maples in autumn dress.

Above: Highway 401, one of many multi-lane freeways in the Toronto area.

Opposite: Acres of pulpwood near Terrace along the north shore of Lake Superior.

Above: The view from one of the numerous lookouts on Manitoulin Island, the largest freshwater island in the world.

Opposite: Fishermen try their luck in a sheltered passageway amidst the Thirty Thousand Islands of Georgian Bay.

Above: The Petrosar Refinery at Sarnia.

Opposite: Canada Day is celebrated at Ontario Place, a summer entertainment complex built on man-made islands along Toronto's waterfront.

Above: Windsurfers on Lake Ontario near Burlington.

Opposite: Dressed in the uniform of the British during the War of 1812, this infantryman demonstrates the art of loading and firing a musket at Fort George, Niagara-on-the-Lake.

Following pages: Skaters on the rink at Nathan Phillips Square in Toronto.

Above: The sun breaks through threatening clouds over Lake Erie.

Opposite: The boardwalk into the marsh at Point Pelee National Park provides the opportunity for watching many species of birds.

Above: The tallest building in the British Commonwealth, first Canadian Place in Toronto catches the light of the setting sun.

Opposite: The City Hall in Kingston.

Above: Winter storm along the Great Lakes.

Opposite: Hundreds of lakes and islands north and west of Lake Superior make an incredible maze of land and water.

Preceding Pages: The lighthouse on Beausoleil Island on Georgian Bay.

Above: A misty evening near Colborne.

Opposite: An aerial view of the Thirty Thousand Islands at sunset.

Above: A wet snowfall outlines trees in High Park, Toronto.

Opposite: A Huron sunset from the south shore of Georgian Bay in Awenda Provincial Park.

Lake of the Woods, near Rainy River.